I0481773

The Credit Card Time Bomb

Deadly Plastic Weapons of Mass Destruction
in the USA, UK, Australia and China

by

Iris Marie Mack, PhD, EMBA

Copyright © 2018 Phat Math, Incorporated

All Rights Reserved.

ISBN-10: 172070337X

ISBN-13: 978-1720703372

Disclaimer

No part of this publication may be reproduced in any form or by any means, including scanning, photocopying, or otherwise without prior written permission of the copyright holders.

The Author has tried to be an authentic source of the information provided in this book. However, she does not oppose the additional information available over the internet or other sources in an updated form.

While all attempts have been made to verify information provided in this publication, the Author assumes no responsibility for errors, omissions, or contrary interpretation of the subject matter herein. Any perceived slights of specific people or organizations are unintentional.

Table of Contents

About the Author

Iris Marie Mack, PhD, EMBA, is an American academic, author, and entrepreneur who has focused on risk management and derivatives products in the energy and financial markets. Dr. Mack has worked for prestigious organizations such as AT&T Bell Labs, MIT, Fitch Learning *Certificate in Quantitative Finance Program* on Wall Street, NASA, and Boeing. More information about Dr. Mack may be found on her Amazon Author page and in her finance and business columns for the International Business Times – UK edition.

Other Books Published by Author Iris Marie Mack, PhD, EMBA

1. *U.S. Debt: $800,000+ Per Family? Trillions? Quadrillions?* (Mack, 2017a)

2. *Wall Street Options Strategy: Everyone Can Learn Covered Calls* (Chinese Edition) (Mack, 2017b)

3. *Rescate de Wall Street Para Main Street: La Estrategia Blindala Que Sera' Bien Pagada* (Spanish Edition) (Mack, 2017c)

4. *A Wall Street Bailout for Main Street: This Bulletproof Trade Will Help You Get Paid* (Mack, 2016)

5. *Energy Trading and Risk Management: A Practical Approach to Hedging, Trading and Portfolio Diversification* (Wiley Finance) 1st Edition (Mack, 2014)

6. *Mama Says, "Money Doesn't Grow on Trees!": World of Dr. Mackamatix* - Mathematics Edutainment Book (Mack, 2011)

7. *Mama Says, "Money Doesn't Grow on Trees!": World of Dr. Mackamatix* - Mathematics Edutainment Book (Mack, 2004)

Introduction

0.1 Credit in Ancient Times

The use of credit in exchange for goods is an ancient concept, which is even mentioned in the Bible as early as Exodus 22:25 where it is written:

> *If thou lend money to any of my people that is poor by thee, thou shalt not be to him as an usurer, neither shalt thou lay upon him usury"* (Holy Bible).

In modern English, *usury* has come to mean *excessive interest upon money loaned, either formally illegal or at least oppressive.* In the Bible, however, the word *usury* simply meant *interest of any kind upon money* (Smith, 2004).

In ancient days in Assyria and Babylon, lending was done by both individuals and banks of merchants which provided grain loans to farmers (for seed) and traders (for trading) as early as 2000 BC. This was later adopted in ancient Greece and Rome where lenders, based in temples, made loans, accepted deposits, and changed money. Archeological evidence of money lending in ancient India and China has also been found (Desjardins, 2017).

0.2 Credit in the Modern Age

0.2.1 Oldest Bank is in Italy

In Europe, credit is particularly mentioned in the play *The Merchant of Venice* by William Shakespeare as far back as the 16th century, in which Antonio owed Shylock and the latter demanded a pound of flesh (Shakespeare, 2015).

The banking system, as we know it today, started in Florence, Genoa, and Venice in the 14th century. The oldest bank today is the Italian bank called *Banca Monte dei Paschi di Siena,* which has operated continuously since 1472 (*Wikipedia1*). Apparently, the first loans, as we know them today, started in Italy. In addition, the word *bank* is derived from the Italian word *banca,* meaning the bench on which money lenders sat at the marketplace (Ross, 2015).

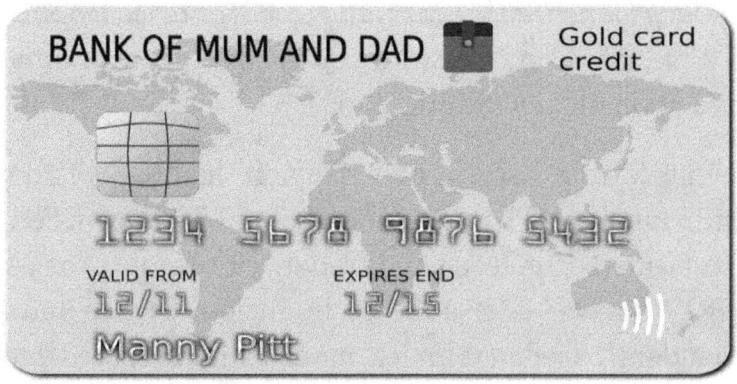

0.2.2 First Credit Cards

According to Britannica.com, the first credit cards were issued to customers by companies in the 1920s, but the first universal credit card was issued by Diners Club, Incorporated in 1950.

The bank credit card system was launched in 1958 when Bank of America issued *BankAmericard,* which was renamed *VISA* around 1976/77 (Encyclopedia Britannica).

Now, the credit card system is global. It's normal for some people to have at least one credit card. Credit cards are convenient because one doesn't need to carry cash around, and they're accepted throughout the world when traveling. This is a great plus for paying hotels, car rental companies, restaurants, and shops far away from home. More importantly, even if a person is broke, he/she can still make important purchases using a credit card, and this is quite useful in an emergency.

0.2.3 Deadly Plastic Weapons of Mass Destruction

As many of us have learned the hard way, the credit card has a nasty side that most people are not aware of when they first get one. Unfortunately for many, credit cards have become *deadly plastic weapons of mass destruction*! Here are few reasons as to why this is the case:

- Many credit cards can end up costing a lot of money in interest charges, which can average over 18% per year in the USA.

- A credit card can give one a false sense of security. It allows cardholders to be careless with their acquisitions, making nonessential purchases on credit, neglecting to pay on time, and then paying high interest rates.

- The issuers of credit cards make so much money in interest that they are keen to get everyone hooked! They make it easy to get a credit card, and some won't even charge interest in the first few months to get users warmed up to the idea of a credit card.

- Even stores issue their own brand of credit cards because they know a lot of people don't pay at the end of the month, so they can charge the cardholders lots of interest.

- Credit card issuers can change the terms of service for the credit cards at any time without consulting with the cardholder, making it easier for cardholders to spiral into heavy debts. This has become such a problem that many households are drowning in debt because of credit cards.

- Many consumers are not aware that the credit card industry is not strictly regulated (Stein, 2004). State laws used to restrict how much a bank in one state could charge customers in another state.

- In 1978, a Supreme Court ruling in the case of Marquette National Bank of Minneapolis v. First of Omaha Service Corp. allowed nationally chartered banks to charge people in other states the interest rate set in the bank's home state. This was the first step towards deregulation (Steiner, 2008).

- At the same time, a number of states seriously needed to improve their economy, so they were quite happy to remove the usury laws. South Dakota was one of those states. In 1980, the Depository Institutions Deregulation and Monetary Control Act called for the complete phase-out of interest rate ceilings on deposit accounts.

- Soon after, other laws were passed to deregulate the financial industry even more (Sherman, 2009). As a result, banks began to move their credit card headquarters to those states that didn't limit interest rates.

0.2.4 Double-Digit Growth of the Credit Card Business

The elimination of usury restrictions paved the way for double-digit growth of the credit card business. By 1990, the number of credit cards issued more than doubled, spending on credit cards increased by more than 500% from $518 to $2,700 per household, and credit card issuers' profits soared as a result. Long after the Federal Reserve had lowered *prime rates*, cardholders were willing to continue paying 18% interest (Stein, 2004).

Definition: Prime Rate

The prime rate is an interest rate determined by individual banks. It is often used as a reference rate (also called the base rate) for many types of loans, including credit card loans and loans to small businesses.

Please note that although the Federal Reserve does not have a direct role in setting the prime rate, many banks choose to set their prime rates based partly on the target level of the federal funds rate (the rate that banks charge each other for short-term loans) established by the Federal Open Market Committee. (Federal Reserve)

0.2.5 Reduction of Monthly Minimum Payments

Another move that changed the credit card industry in the 1990s was the reduction of minimum payments. The reduction of the monthly minimum payment benefited the card issuers in two ways.

- First, by paying less per month, credit cardholders will take longer to pay off the balances. Meanwhile, each dollar of the principal generates more income for the card issuers. Such ballooning balances are caused by compound interests, late fees, etc. (Mack, 2011).

- Second, card issuers can increase the credit limit while the consumer continues to pay the same minimum amount.

Between 1990 and 2004, the average U.S. household credit card debt tripled from $2,500 to $7,500 (Stein, 2004). In June 2018, the average U.S. balance-carrying household credit card debt was $9,333, and the total U.S. household credit card debt was approximately $1.03 trillion – larger than the gross domestic product (GDP) of many countries (ValuePenguin, 2018). So it's an understatement to say that banks and retailers make huge profits from their credit card businesses.

Please note that the calculation of average credit card debt always yields different numbers, depending on what is being considered. For example, "average household credit card debt" takes the number of all households into account and the "balance-carrying household credit card debt" takes into account only households that have balances on their credit cards.

0.3 The M.I.T. PhD Mathematician Behind Credit Card Lending Practices

The credit card business is lucrative for lenders, with interest rates far higher than any other loans. The current practice by credit card lenders is the brainchild of Dr. Andrew Kahr - a 1960 Harvard University graduate. Dr. Kahr finished his undergraduate degree at Harvard in three years. In 1962, he earned a PhD in mathematics at the Massachusetts Institute of Technology, aka M.I.T. (*Wikipedia2*). For his contributions to the credit card industry, Kahr was featured in the PBS Frontline documentary *Secret History of the Credit Card* (Frontline, 2004).

As discussed in this very interesting PBS documentary, many financially illiterate people became hooked on credit cards after Dr. Kahr persuaded lenders to:

- Change 18% annual interest rate to 1.5% monthly rate, which people perceive to be far less.

- Charge cardholders 0% interest in the first few months. This adjustable interest suddenly changes to a high interest rate when the consumer revolves a balance.

- Reduce the monthly minimum payment from 5% to 2%, knowing that debts will be owed for a longer time, bringing in more interest.

- Make sure that credit card payment due dates fall on Sundays and holidays so that more people default and have to pay interest (McAleenan, 2014).

Andrew Kahr was instrumental in changing the credit card business from loss-making to excessively profitable. With his financial engineering strategies, it's easy for credit card issuers to lure consumers with a zero percent interest rate and the very low 2% monthly minimum payment. It's easy for desperate consumers to fail to pay the full amount owed on a credit card and to, therefore, revolve the balance and pay interest every month. Most consumers are unaware of any potential problems with their credit cards until they owe too much and cannot service the debt. This is the main reason why credit card issuers aren't overly concerned about defaults.

0.4 Overview of the Book

In this book, we take a peek into the credit card situation in the USA, the UK, Australia, and China. We also provide references for further reading and study. The structure of the chapters in this book is as follows:

Chapter 1: The Credit Card Situation in the USA

Outstanding Credit Card Debt in the USA Was Over 1 Trillion Dollars the Whole of 2017, High Interest Rates, Outstanding U.S. Credit Card Debt in 2017 and 2018, The Credit Card Time Bomb, Understanding Credit Cards, General Purpose and Private Label Retail Credit Cards, Shapes and Sizes of Credit Card Interest Rates, Revolving Credit Card Balance, How Credit Card Debt Affects the U.S. Economy, The Economic Situation in the USA, Credit Card Securitization

Chapter 2: Credit Card Situation in Other Major Economies

Credit Card Debt in the UK, Deadly Plastic Weapons of Mass Destruction Driving People To Commit Suicide, What is Government Doing About It?, Debt Charities, Credit

Card Debt in Australia, Australians' Personal Debt Keeps Increasing, The Credit Card Time Bomb, Government's Response To The Australian Credit Card Debt Crisis, Emerging Credit Card Market In China, Chinese Millenials Have Adopted The Credit Card Lifestyle, The Chinese National Debt, How Chinese Lenders Manage The Credit Card Debt Risk

Chapter 3: The Fear of the Credit Bubble Burst

Analyzing the Credit Bubble Burst of 2008, The Emergence Of Subprime Lending Created A Bubble, The Housing Bubble Burst, Banks Were Affected, The Signs Of Trouble Were Ignored, Securitization Of Mortgage Loans Hid Their Weaknesses, Mortgage Defaults and Collapse of Some Banks, Alarming Factors for the Credit Card Bubble, Factors for the Credit Card Bubble in the USA, Factors for the Credit Card Bubble in the UK, Australia and China, The Bursting Point, American Debt As High Now As It Was At Height of 2008 Credit Bubble, Global Debt Time Bombs

Chapter 4: Credit Card Debt Relief Solutions

Credit Card Delinquency, Debt Consolidation, Debt Consolidation Loan, Debt Management Plan, Do It Yourself Consolidation, Debt Negotiation, Bankruptcy, Chapter 7 (of the Bankruptcy Code), Chapter 13 (of the Bankruptcy Code), Key Things to Know About the Bankruptcy Process, Managing Your Credit Card Debt to Avoid Delinquency, Outright Cancellation of 100% Unsecured Debt, Stricter Credit Limits

Chapter 1:
The Credit Card Situation in the USA

The credit card is very convenient for consumers, especially during times of emergencies. It's easy to carry around and it's payable at the end of the month. Unfortunately, the easy availability of credit cards has increased spending power for some people who may lack self-control. This has landed too many people in financial trouble, forcing them into bankruptcy, repossessions, homelessness, and/or lowering their overall standards of living.

1.1 Outstanding Credit Card Debt in the USA Was Over 1 Trillion Dollars the Whole of 2017!

1.1.1 High Interest Rates

Credit cards have become a way of life for many Americans, and they have managed to become an easy source of debt despite the high interest rates. Some consumers continue to use credit cards with high interest rates in spite of the availability of lower interest bank loans that some of them may qualify for (Luthi, 2017).

1.1.2 Outstanding U.S. Credit Card Debt in 2017 and 2018

The Federal Reserve revealed that revised December 2016 figures (reported in January 2017) indicated that credit card debt topped $1 trillion then (Kilpatrick, 2017). It remained above $1 trillion the whole of 2017. As previously stated in the Introduction, in June 2018 the total U.S. household credit card debt was approximately $1.03 trillion. Some experts even view this continued increase in credit card debt to be a good sign for the U.S. economy (Andriotis, 2017), (Golle, 2017).

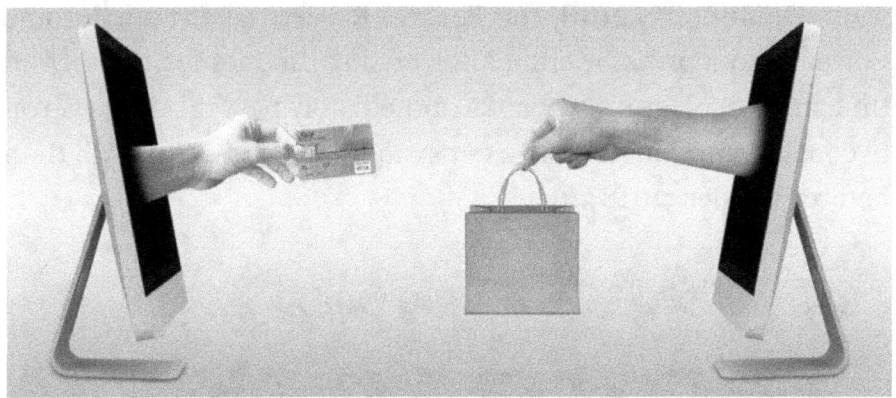

But is the increase in credit card debt really a good sign for the American economy? At 18% interest rate (average) consumers pay banks and stores $15 billion in interest every month! Credit card issuers are creaming it every month! This is probably the easiest money that lenders make out of consumers without even pushing them to consume. Exceeding $1 trillion in credit card debt is definitely good for the card issuers. This good fortune for lenders may not last forever. Even though there are signs that the U.S. economy is gaining some steam under President Trump, many Americans are still defaulting on credit cards due to job losses, high cost of living, and other unforeseen circumstances. (Mack, 2017a), (FRED, 2018)

In 2017 the average credit card debt for U.S. householders was approximately $8,377 (Elkins, 2017). Hence, at an average interest rate of 16.06% per annum, households paid an average of $112.11 in interest per month or $1,345.35 per year (Dilworth, 2017). As previously stated in the Introduction, in June 2018, the average U.S. balance-carrying household credit card debt was $9,333, That is a lot of money to pay for credit card debt, especially for many low- and middle-income households! (Rounds, 2018)

Already, the Federal Reserve hiked interest rates several times in 2017. On June 13, 2018, the Federal Reserve Chairman Jerome Powell held a press briefing after raising the rate for the second time in 2018. Naturally, banks immediately pass this increase on to consumers, who now have to pay more interest per month than before (Dickler, 2018).

1.2 The Credit Card Time Bomb

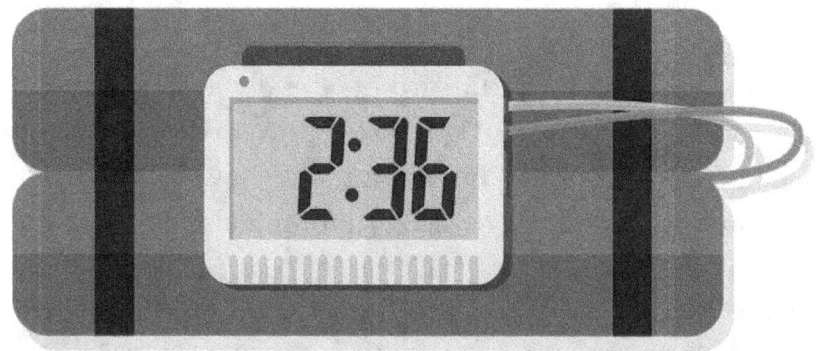

Over 157 million Americans owe on one or more credit cards (Dickler, 2017). In June 2018, these consumers had $1.03 trillion in outstanding credit card debt. This exceeded the record $1.02 trillion in April 2008 during the big economic crash (Lamagna, 2017). Is the USA headed for a credit card bubble?

The rapid increase in credit card debt in the USA has been blamed on unemployment, underemployment, and family income that has been increasing slowly (if at all) in the last decade but has failed to keep up with inflation over the same period (Mack, 2016, 2017a). Households that are unable to meet their living expenses use credit cards for major expenses like rent and mortgage payments (Dickler, 2017). Another reason for credit card debt in the USA is that lenders are issuing cards to people with below-average credit scores, increasing the number of credit cardholders to 171 million in 2017 and 134 million in 2018. Then there are those people who are shopaholics. They will shop even when they don't need to. (Lamagna, 2017), (Rounds, 2018)

As discussed in the previous section, interest rates were increased several times in 2017 and 2018. How long can the credit card consumers continue to meet their obligations, especially if the interest rates on their credit cards keep increasing? Being so highly indebted, consumers are very vulnerable to higher interest rates and any other small changes in the economy right now.

As early as July 2016, there were all the obvious signs that the United States was about to enter into a recession. The poor job situation and the increases in debt meant that lenders faced a high risk of bad debts as consumers failed to pay. What happened on the stock market, in the housing market, and in the credit card industry since the 2008 market collapse indicates that another recession could be on the way (Amadeo, 2017a). Unfortunately, another recession will naturally reduce credit card debtors' ability to pay their debts. It's a *time bomb* that could implode any day now.

Please note that recent jobs reports and relatively low unemployment numbers for certain segments of the U.S. population indicate that there has been some short-term improvement in the U.S. economy (Schoen, 2018). However, U.S. consumers' total credit debt still exceeds $1.03 trillion (Pak, 2018). Hence, to err on the side of caution, it makes sense to get rid of credit card debt.

1.3 Understanding Credit Cards

Credit cards are the modern way of borrowing. Let's take a look at the various types of credit cards and also the different levels of credit card interest rates.

1.3.1 General Purpose and Private Label Retail Credit Cards

The lender is the issuer of the card. There are two types of credit cards lenders can issue, namely:

- The *general purpose card* that one may use for anything anywhere.
- The *private label retail card* that can only be used at the outlets owned by the issuer of the card (e.g., a retail store or service station).

Most general purpose credit cards are **unsecured**, meaning that they are issued based on a person's credit history. It's possible to have **secured** credit cards that are secured by funds held in a deposit account, which the card issuer can access if the borrower fails to pay. Private label retail credit cards generally charge more interest than general purpose cards (Sandberg, 2017).

1.3.2 Shapes and Sizes of Credit Card Interest Rates

Credit card interest rates come in various shapes and sizes:

- From as low as 0% interest rate
- To as high as 30% interest rate
- And even a **limited-balance transfer rate,** the amount that a cardholder is allowed to transfer to a new card at a special interest rate that's lower than the standard rate

Please note that the annual interest rate that a consumer is charged is determined by

- Income
- Credit score
- Assets
- Current debt load
- Credit inquiries
- Payment history
- Economic conditions

Consumers with positive and proven credit histories are charged the lowest interest rates (Sandberg, 2017).

1.3.3 Revolving Credit Card Balance

Do you ever wonder what happens behind the scenes when you make a purchase for goods and services with your credit card? Well, each time you make a purchase with your credit card, the following happens:

1. The purchase information is sent to the issuer.
2. The issuer makes the payment on your behalf.
3. The issuer records the loan against your account.
4. This loan amount is added to your existing balance.
5. If you pay off the balance on or before the due date, you're not charged interest.
6. If you make only the minimum payment, you can carry over the balance to the following month and you're charged interest on that outstanding balance.

Not paying part of the loan is called **revolving** the balance. Meanwhile, you can buy more goods and service with the remaining buying power of your credit card (Sandberg, 2017).

1.3.4 How Credit Card Debt Affects the U.S. Economy

Let's take a quick look at the pros and cons of credit card usage and how it affects the economy:

The Pros of Credit Card Usage: In theory, credit cards can be good for the U.S. economy. The credit card gives consumers buying power that they might not otherwise have. This provides businesses with revenue that they might not have if people didn't have a credit card. Retailers, travel agencies, auto parts shops, and other in-demand businesses rely on consumer credit card purchases in order to survive and provide jobs for their employees. With increased revenue, businesses continue to make or buy goods and they keep people employed. Hence, credit cards help to stimulate the economy. In fact, personal consumer spending (which includes credit card spending) accounts for more than two-thirds of the U.S. gross domestic product (GDP; *Discover*, 2017).

The Cons of Credit Card Usage: There's a limit to the positive effects that credit cards can have on the economy. When cardholders incur too much debt, they use up their buying power and end up having less spending ability. Their failure to buy goods can hurt the economy. If interest rates keep increasing, they can eventually reduce consumers' ability to make new purchases, and the economy suffers (*Discover*, 2017).

Credit cards may also lead to an increase in inflation. Retailers increase prices of goods when demand for the goods increase. By purchasing goods that they would otherwise not afford, consumers increase demand for those goods, prompting retailers and manufacturers to increase prices. Also, even if the price of particular goods remained the same, consumers who buy on credit end up paying more for those goods through interest charges, and that erodes consumers' buying power (Randall, 2010).

When consumers start defaulting on their credit card payments, bankers have two ways of recovering their money.

- First, they may find ways to hike bank fees charged to other bank customers to make up for lost interest and principal. So other people are made to pay for the sins of credit card defaulters.

- Second, banks may get a bailout from the U.S. government as they did after the 2008 economic crisis. Ultimately, this bailout comes out of U.S. taxpayers' pockets (Mack, 2016; Leuthold, 2017).

1.4 The Economic Situation in the USA

Many credit cardholders are defaulting on their card payments. According to a report by Business Insider, published on June 9,

2017, in the two fiscal quarters ending March 2017, banks reported a sharp increase in credit card charge-offs — uncollectable debts written off. It's suspected that the defaults are due to lower standards of lending (Morrell, 2017). Almost a year later on May 21, 2018 Business Insider later reported that more Americans still struggled to pay off their credit cards and that late payments on credit card debt remains on the rise (Oyedele, 2018).

However, credit card default is most likely linked to:

- The real unemployment rate that is higher than the official unemployment rate. In May 2018, the number of people not in U.S. workforce increased by another 170,000 – rising to 95.915 million people (Durden, 2018). Hence, while more people are reported to be employed now in the United States, many of them are part-time because they cannot find full time employment. Others have been so long out of their regular high paying jobs that they can't get back to the professional level they attained in the past. Therefore, they settle for lower paying jobs.

- Due to lengthy periods of unemployment, many people eventually give up looking for work. Those who drop off the unemployment rolls are simply no longer factored into the real unemployment rate (Mack, 2016).

- Apparently, many job openings are in low-paying retail and food service industries. In real terms, structural unemployment has increased, making the real unemployment rate probably double the reported rate (Amadeo, 2017b; Mack, 2016).

- The interest rates that the Federal Reserve Bank keeps increasing, a cost that the banks pass on to consumers, increase cardholders' credit card debt even further.

High unemployment rate coupled with increasing interest rates simply make it difficult for consumers to service their credit card debt, leading more and more to default. This cannot be good for the lenders and the consumers. Does relief exist for both? We will discuss some relief options for credit cardholders in the final chapter of this book.

1.5 Credit Card Securitization

Credit card issuers manage part of their risk by ***securitizing credit card debts***. Securitization essentially involves the pooling together of credit card receivables. These receivables are then sold to trusts who then sell them to third party investors as *Asset Backed Securities* (ABS). By securitizing the debts, lenders realize an immediate cash flow and reduce risk of default. With this option available to them, they just merrily keep issuing more credit cards (Choudhry & Baig, 2013).

Chapter 2:
The Credit Card Situation in Other Major Economies

Credit cards are common in most countries, even in the Third World. However, consumer behavior varies from country to country (Konsko, 2014). For example,

- Canadians tend to pay off their purchases at the end of the month.

- The French have a culture of saving about 10% of income, so they charge very little to their credit cards.

- The use of credit cards is rising in China and Brazil, whose economies have been growing for a long time.

- Use of credit cards in the UK and Australia is similar to the American way.

2.1 Credit Card Debt in the UK

As of April 2017, Britons owed 68.1 billion pounds on credit cards, a 9.7% increase on the 2016 debt levels (Giles, 2017). By the end of January 2018, Britons had 70.35 billion pounds in credit card debts (Quinn, 2018).

The Bank of England is already worried that, should there be a recession, lenders will lose a lot of money due to credit card defaults. Presently, bad consumer debts account for roughly 10% of all bad debts, which banks write off. It's said that one of the reasons this is happening is that lenders are offering longer interest-free periods in an effort to lure consumers to get credit cards and use them (Wallace, 2017a). Is anybody across the pond in the UK worried about the consumers who are defaulting?

The average household in the UK owed unsecured debts amounting to £13,200 at the end of 2016, just below the £13,300 level at the end of 2008, on the eve of the credit crunch. Most of the household debts have been financed by credit card purchases. As of March 2017, households owed an extra £1.6 billion in consumer debts, at least a 10% increase compared to the same time the previous year. All this happened despite rising inflation and slow wage growth. In other words, credit cards seem to keep people going when they can't afford purchases of goods and services (Wallace, 2017b). If people are using credit cards to close the gap between income and needs, then this cannot be sustainable.

A Reuters poll on December 29, 2016 indicated that economists expected UK economic growth in 2017 to decrease by more than 50% to a rate of 1.1%, while inflation would rise to almost 3% compared to 0% in January 2016 (Inman, 2017). Obviously, United Kingdom credit card consumers are very vulnerable and may be affected by any small changes in the economy. Many consumers might be unable to service their credit card debt and lenders might lose around £18.5 billion on their books in the event of a major economic crisis (Chan, 2017).

In July 2017, the Bank of England, which was worried about another financial crisis, sternly warned lenders that they risk legal action for reckless lending. The Bank of England acknowledged that terms and conditions on credit cards and personal loans had become too easy, with the following very attractive conditions:

- Advertised 0% interest period extended to 30 months
- Advertised interest rates reduced from 8% to 3.8% even though official interest rates had barely changed.

Though credit card issuers didn't seem to worry about such ridiculous terms, the Bank of England saw the risks for lenders, consumers, and the economy as a whole (Elliott, 2017).

Though lenders kept issuing credit cards, the rate of credit card delinquency rose to 2.47% in the second quarter of 2017, compared to 2.2% in the previous year (Subba & Lahiri, 2017). Obviously, lenders make so much money from each consumer that the loss from default is small compared to the gains. And while one consumer is defaulting, several new consumers are getting caught in the credit card net. Therefore, lenders cannot be expected to change their lending practices without being forced to. Another reason why lenders aren't too worried is that, as previously discussed in Section 1.5, they securitize credit card debts and pass on the risk to investors.

2.1.1 Deadly Plastic Weapons of Mass Destruction Driving People to Suicide

While the Central Bank and economists worry about the effects of the rising credit card debts on the economy, there is a hidden cost to the nation that's hardly ever acknowledged. People in the UK are becoming overwhelmed with debt and they are committing suicide because their debt is out of control and they cannot service it any more.

How can a financial system issue more than £100,000 in credit card spending limits to people who earn very modest salaries? In the BBC Documentary *"The Money Trap: How Banks Control the World Through Debt,"* a whistleblower explains what's really happening (*BBC*, 2012).

i. Banks and retail stores flood consumers with dozens of credit card offers daily. Even worse, they are, oftentimes, intentionally issuing credit cards to people who are desperate for money and are easily tempted.

ii. Armed with more buying power, consumers spend on things that they normally wouldn't spend on.

iii. Most consumers become **revolvers** – that is, they pay the minimum required each month and they revolve the balance forward.

iv. Revolvers are the favorites of the banks and retailers because they pay a lot of interest on their balances every month.

v. Lenders incentivize consumers by giving them unsolicited credit limit increases and giving them gold or platinum status to make them spend more.

vi. Within a short time, consumers juggle many cards from various lenders and they're overindebted.

vii. Eventually, most of the consumers' income goes to paying the minimum plus interest every month.

viii. While demanding payments from defaulters, the lenders increase credit limits. It's a very vicious and deadly trap!

ix. Desperate and not seeing a way out, some consumers commit suicide, hoping that the debt will go away. Unfortunately, many lenders keep trying to collect from the bereaved family, even after the death of the desperate borrower (*BBC*, 2012).

Let's put this into perspective. A person owing £100,000 on 7 credit cards at an average of 5% interest per annum – is charged £416 in interest per month plus the 2% minimum payments on each card, say £285 each totaling £2,000. The cardholder must pay a total of £2,416 per month! Depending on the person's take home income, there's barely any left after paying the credit card debt. Obviously, this person has to use credit cards again to make it to the end of the next month. Please note for purposes of illustration we used an average of 5% per annum because earlier in Section 2.1 we stated that lenders lure consumers by offering interest rates as low as 3.8%. However, in reality, the interest rate rates can be much higher. As a matter of fact, in November 2017 the average credit card interest rates in the UK was 23%. (Milligan, 2017).

These deadly plastic weapons of mass destruction are driving people to commit suicide. Sadly, there are many cases of reported suicide due to credit card debt, such as:

- A father of two who committed suicide because he owed £70,000 on 19 credit cards (Barrow, 2004).

- A bank worker who owed £100,000 committed suicide (Daily Mail Reporter, 2006).

These are just two examples out of many confirmed suicides due to credit card debts. Who knows how many other unconfirmed desperate people have committed suicide due to exorbitant amounts of credit card debts. Apparently, suicide is contemplated by 50% of indebted Britons. The good thing is that help is available and debt relief options exist (Debt Support Trust).

2.1.2 What is Government Doing About It?

The Bank of England has taken an interest in the matter of credit cards and other loans. It has instructed UK banks to raise their capital ratios as a preventive step in case there's an economic slowdown (Amaro, 2017).

Both Labour and the Tories have committed to adopt a "breathing space" policy that will enable payments for distressed borrowers to be frozen and replaced by a statutory payment plan. Meanwhile, the Financial Conduct Authority (FCA) is investigating credit card lending, and it has created a host of rules to help struggling people. This includes ordering lenders to waive, reduce, or cancel interest and charges in some dire cases (Warwick-Ching, 2017).

2.1.3 Debt Charities

More British people are seeking financial assistance to make ends meet. For example, in 2016, around 600,000 people approached StepChange, the UK's leading debt charity. StepChange says millions of Britons are seeking help, and it estimates that 8.8 million Britons have turned to debt to pay for daily household expenses (Warwick-Ching, 2017).

2.2 Credit Card Debt in Australia

The use of credit cards is very common in Australia. The total debt owed increased from AU$5.9 billion in 1995 to AU$52 billion in 2017 on 16.7 million credit cards (Emmerton, 2017). However, for some consumers, credit cards have led to a downward financial spiral.

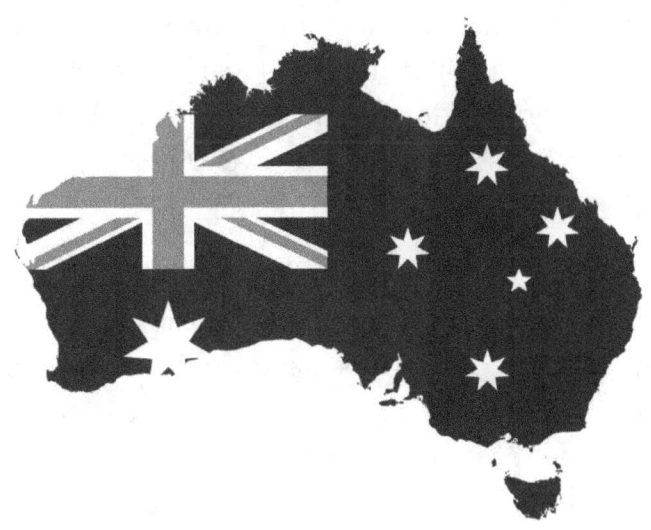

The prices of gas and electricity and other services continue to rise while wages are rising too slowly. As a result, many Australians were in financial distress in 2017. Those who manage to make mortgage payments do so by ignoring other debts or by paying for expenses with credit cards.

According to Digital Finance Analytics, 1% of Australian households are in severe financial stress, meaning that they're behind with their debt payments. Such people are trying to find their way out of debt by either selling their properties, refinancing, and/or seeking help from services like National Debt Helpline. Unfortunately, people in financial distress often seek assistance from crooked credit card companies and payday lenders first, only to find themselves in a worse situation a few weeks later. Then they may seek help from debt counselors (Taylor, 2017).

2.2.1 Australians' Personal Debt Keeps Increasing

In 2017 Australia ranked fourth (behind Denmark, the Netherlands and Norway) in the world in terms of personal debt as a percentage of income. Australians owe more than 210% of household income for housing loans, car loans, investor loans, student loans, personal loans, and credit cards (Finder3, 2017). In total, Australians owed lenders over AU$2 trillion in 2017 (McCulloch, 2017).

About 92.8% of the AU$2 trillion was owed for houses and investments, which sounds healthy on the surface. Low interest rates on houses have made repayments more affordable. However, with an average debt to income ratio of 88%, a small increase in interest rates and a decline in home prices can make it difficult for people to make debt payments or to sell and make a profit. Compared to the national average, some households owe much more and are experiencing more repayment stress. Unfortunately, those are the ones who are now at the mercy of dodgy credit cards and payday lenders (Finder1, 2017).

Australians are heavily investing in property because they fear that their pensions may not be worth very much when they reach retirement age. Due to the increased demand for real estate, house prices are very high, and keep increasing. However, investors keep borrowing to buy more properties in the hope that they'll make a lot of money on reselling the properties.

Unfortunately, the market is flooded and too many of these properties are empty. Yet each property is used as collateral for the next purchase, done in the hope that property prices will remain high or will keep increasing. Banks, on the other hand, keep issuing interest-only loans in which borrowers pay only the interest for up to 7 years. Interest-only loans make borrowers feel that they can afford repayments, forgetting that they're simply postponing principal repayments. Some refinance after 7 years and never pay off the principal. It's a huge gamble (Wood, 2016).

Seems Australians have a house of cards on their hands that may come tumbling down any time. If home prices start falling, too many investors will be paying a lot of money for worthless properties. If interest rates go up at the same time, then people won't be able to afford servicing for all the loans, including credit card debt (Wood, 2016).

2.2.2 The Credit Card Debt Time Bomb

"Bad debts" such as credit cards make up a small proportion of personal loans in Australia. However, in 2016, Australians owed a total of AU$51 billion in credit card debt with AU$32.5 billion of that in revolving debt. They paid at least AU$5 billion in interest (Wood, 2016). In 2017, Australians owed AU$31.7 billion in interest-bearing credit card debt and were paying AU$5.4 billion in interest for the year, estimated at 17.22% per annum. This translates to an average of AU$4,215.89 in credit card debt per cardholder who pays at least AU$700 in interest every year (MoneySmart, 2017). Unfortunately, some Australians owe as much as AU$150,000 in credit card debt! It's a credit card time bomb in Australia!

Victoria's Consumer Action Law Center has claimed that about 50% of the people who contact them for help owe over AU$10,000 in credit card debt, and every week, they get at least one person owing more than AU$100,000 (Janda, 2016). They also have found that:

- Some people use one credit card to pay off the minimum repayment on another credit card, which they can sustain for a short period before it, too, doesn't work.

- People are being approved for mortgage loans even though their earnings are not sufficient.

- When they borrow money to buy a house, consumers get a compulsory credit card with a limit of AU$23,000, which they end up using to pay the mortgage.

- When they come for help, about 25% of the people who get compulsory credit cards with their housing loans have already lost their houses after using credit cards to try to pay for their home loans.

- Some people owe more than 150% of their annual salary in credit card debt (Janda, 2016).

- About 80% of people aged 55 and over have a credit card, and about 18% of people in that age group have three or more credit cards (Finder2). Even people on government pension (welfare) can owe as much as AU$80,000 on credit cards.

- Some consumers hold two or three cards with the same credit card lender or can owe one credit card lender up to AU$40,000.

- Loan consolidation by banks is increasing as banks help their clients to consolidate their personal loans. It's a simple shift from one form of loan (credit card) to another (the consolidated loan). This is how credit card debt figures have appeared to decline in Australia.

Basically, the Consumer Action Law Center has found corrupt lending practices by the financial industry. Now the credit card debt in Australia is a ticking time bomb because a slight change in the economy can cause mass defaults on credit cards, affecting lenders and cardholders.

2.2.3 Government's Response to the Australian Credit Card Debt Crisis

In response to the ticking time bomb, the Australian treasurer, Scott Morrison, proposed the following four reforms in 2017.

- An affordability assessment will look at the customer's "ability to repay the full credit limit within a reasonable period" before issuing a card.

- The Australian government now forbids unsolicited offers of credit limit increases.

- The methodology for interest calculations must be explained to consumers.

- Cancelling a card or reducing a limit online must be made easier.

Mr. Morrison said each Australian is responsible for managing his/her credit card debt. However, he also acknowledges that most people are not aware of the implication of their actions when they make only the minimum monthly payments (Emmerton, 2017).

2.3 Emerging Credit Card Market in China

Credit cards were first introduced to China in 1985. In 2017, the number of credit cards issued in China was estimated to be between 600 and 700 million cards (John, 2017). In 2014, MasterCard projected that annual credit card spending in China will more than double by 2025 with China becoming the largest credit card market in the world by number of issued cards, overtaking the United States (Hart, Kidd, Rettig, & Walker, 2014).

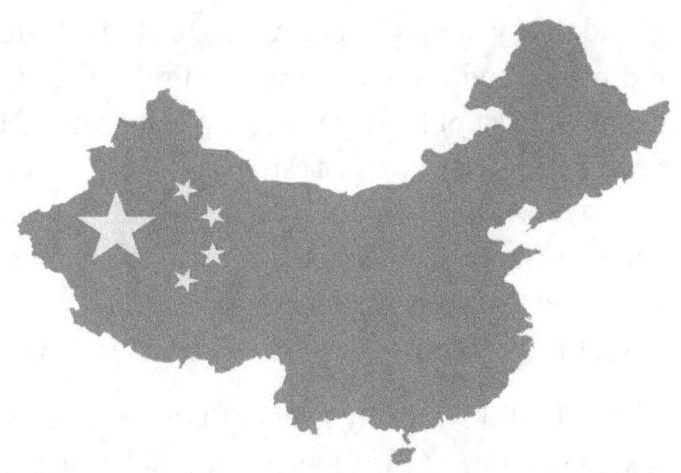

2.3.1 Chinese Millenials Have Adopted the Credit Card Lifestyle!

To older Chinese people who were taught to save, borrowing is shameful. However, the Chinese people are being encouraged to create credit histories and they are borrowing to do just that (*The Economist,* 2016). That move has encouraged the Chinese millenials, the newly rising middle class, also known as the Moonlight Generation, to use credit cards. They're under 35 years old and include urban students and professionals who don't live according to tradition. They're called Moonlight Generation because they spend all their salaries on goods and services and their bank accounts are light at the end of the month. The Moonlight Generation is very much sophisticated in their tastes. They particularly like the luxury brands of the West and they don't mind using their credit cards for online purchases. Because major online shopping platforms such as Alibaba and JD.com now offer popular buy-now-pay-later deals, these young Chinese people are seriously hooked on their credit cards (Global Blue).

It's not just the creation of credit history that's causing credit card debt. Banks aggressively market credit cards by offering rewards, discounts, and lucky draws. They give credit cards to young unemployed people and some have reported receiving unsolicited cards in the mail. Most of these young people are responsible, but there's a small but growing group of card "slaves" who end up losing control over their spending in order to maintain "face" among friends and colleagues. A weakness that research has found among young Chinese is the need to display wealth, which leads to revolving credit card debt, eventually leading to debt slavery (Hart et al., 2014).

Credit card use is still relatively new in China. Hence, currently only approximately 14% of the Chinese cardholders are revolvers (Changzheng, Zhua, Zhanga, & Heb, 2016). Unfortunately, it's difficult for some people to control credit card use. As a result, some Chinese consumers are already struggling to pay credit card debt. In 2016, the total overdue credit card debt (over 60 days old) was 48 billion yuan (US $7.2 billion), just over 1.4% of the total credit card debt of 3.4 trillion yuan or US $514.2 billion (*PYMNTS*, 2016).

In 2014, three members of a family committed suicide when they failed to pay their credit card debt of approximately $1,204 – a fortune in China (Watson, 2014). How long before the Chinese credit card bubble bursts? Currently, the credit card problem, on its own, might not look like a huge problem, but it's part of an even bigger problem, the Chinese national debt.

2.3.2 The Chinese National Debt

Following the economic meltdown of 2008 in the West, China went on to borrow heavily to build cities and roads, to invest and to strengthen its economy. Now the country is heavily indebted, with corporate debt standing at 100% of GDP in 2008 and 170% of GDP in 2016 (Macfarlane, 2017a). In the first quarter of 2017, total debt to GDP ratio rose to 304% (Amaro, 2017). Since 2005, China has accounted for 50% of all new credit created globally, yet its economy only accounts for about 15% of the global economy (Smith, 2017).

In May 2017, Moody's Investors Service downgraded China's sovereign debt one notch to A1, the agency's fifth-highest rating (Macfarlane, 2017b). Is the next global financial crisis going to start with a Chinese sovereign debt default?

If anything goes wrong with the Chinese economy, it will affect the international lenders, international trade, and unemployment rates. Consumers who lose their jobs will default on their credit card debts at a higher rate. It appears that the Chinese national debt has potential to trigger the burst of the credit card bubble in China.

2.3.3 How Chinese Lenders Manage the Credit Card Debt Risk

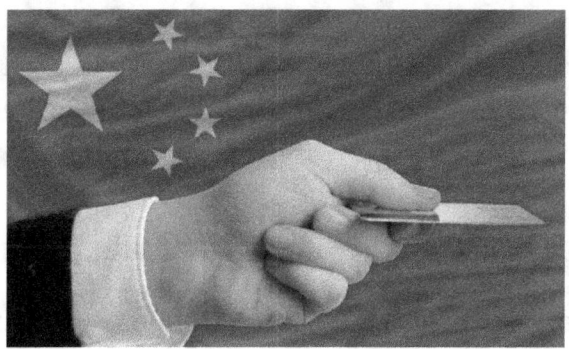

Banks in China have started to securitize nonperforming loans. This way, Chinese banks quickly improve their cashflow while passing on the risk of default to investors (Li, 2017). When the credit cardholders pay back the loan, they pay to these investors through their banks.

Chapter 3:
The Fear of the Credit Bubble Burst

Various articles have been written about a possible credit bubble burst. But there's no consensus on that, and the authorities are very quiet on the matter. We'll look at the situation that led to the financial meltdown of 2008 and see if we're facing a similar situation now.

3.1 Analyzing the Credit Bubble Burst of 2008

The bubbles that burst in the USA in 2008 were real estate and derivatives bubbles. The Federal Reserve had gradually lowered the Fed Fund Rate to only 1.24% by November 2002, encouraging more people to afford interest payments on their mortgages.

3.1.1 The Emergence of Subprime Lending Created a Bubble

Low interest rates caused demand for houses to increase as more people could afford the repayments. As a result, house prices increased and kept increasing, eventually peaking in 2006. But then house prices began to decline in 2007. Meanwhile, due to deregulation of the financial industry, banks were engaged in speculative trading with derivatives and the issuance of interest-only loans to subprime borrowers (Amadeo, 2017c; Mack, 2016).

By 2006, consumers with less than perfect credit ratings made up 20% of the U.S. housing market. Apparently, some banks made subprime lending their major business (*Investopedia1,* 2016). By 2007, the subprime mortgages had grown into a trillion-dollar industry as new homeowners demanded more houses, which real estate developers tried to build.

3.1.2 The Housing Bubble Burst

In 2004, the Federal Reserve started to raise interest rates. By June 2006, the interest rate was 5.25% and the subprime homeowners began to default on payments (Amadeo, 2017c). Demand for houses began to decline, leading to decline of house prices in 2007.

House prices began to fall as homeowners failed to pay and tried to sell. But demand had gone down and no one was buying. By December 30, 2008, house prices hit an all-time low. As a result of the bursting real estate bubble, banks refused to lend money, causing a credit crisis, which resulted in a recession (*PositiveMoney*).

3.1.3 Banks Were Affected

In early 2008, banks experienced too many late payments and loan defaults, hence causing some of the banks to collapse. Insurance companies such as AIG that had insured most of these mortgages were affected. Mortgage loans that had been securitized began to default. Institutions such as Lehman Brothers and Bear Sterns that underwrote, owned, and sold many of these investments, experienced such a huge drop in value that they had to shut their businesses while bringing down other businesses. The increased number of foreclosures began to bring down values of nearby homes. The chain reaction spread across the USA from 2008 to 2010 (*Investopedia1*, 2016).

3.1.4 The Signs of Trouble Were Ignored

This collapse of the housing market wasn't sudden. There were signs of a housing bubble and derivatives bubbles as early as 2001. I saw this coming and went on record to call such a collapse far back when I was at Enron and later at Harvard Management Company. To the chagrin of some of my former bosses, I expressed my concerns about volatile derivatives securities that played a major role in the 2008 market crash. However, these are topics for other books (Hartmann, 2009).

In addition, many economists over the years wrote about the housing bubble. Simultaneously, just as many prominent and authoritative economists threw water over the problem, claiming that there was no problem at all. Therefore, ordinary investors who bought houses those days cannot be faulted for taking actions that unwittingly fueled the bubble and suffered the disastrous consequences for themselves and the nation (Bartlett, 2009). The same can be said about the investors who bought derivatives securities – aka financial *weapons of mass destruction* – as referred to by billionaire investor Warren Buffett (Shen, 2016; Influential Individuals, 2017).

3.1.5 Securitization of Mortgage Loans Hid their Weaknesses

Even institutional investors were affected because the real risks were hidden when mortgage loans were securitized and turned into AAA (least risky) rated securities. Here's how it worked:

- Investment banks bought thousands of mortgages from lenders.

- These mortgages were then packaged into "tranches." Please note that a **tranche** is a group of loans with the same risk profile.

- Credit rating agencies ranked these tranches according to risk, with AAA rating meaning a tranche had the lowest risk. Senior tranches, which had the lowest risk, made up approximately 80% of the securities and every investor trusted the credit rating agencies' ranking of these securities.

- These tranches were then sold onto investors.

- Borrowers getting interest-only loans thought they could pay them back comfortably so they bought houses.

- Because the lenders did not have to hold those loans, they stopped worrying about quality and kept issuing more housing loans even to subprime borrowers.

- The investment banks didn't worry about quality either, seeing that one default wouldn't impact on the quality of the pool of mortgages.

- Because of the AAA rating, investors like pension funds, large banks, individuals, and hedge funds believed these securities to be safe, so they invested in them (Holt, 2009).

Although many investors took the risk of default, some were covered by insurance, known as **credit default swaps**, sold by large insurance companies such as AIG. Investors felt safe and snapped up the derivatives securities (Amadeo, 2017c).

3.1.6 Mortgage Defaults and Collapse of Some Banks

Too many defaults in the early part of 2008 made the mortgage investments lose value, leading to the collapse of some investment banks. After a series of events that led to heavy losses and decline of bank share prices, Lehman Brothers filed for bankruptcy on September 15, 2008. They held $619 billion in debt and their assets were worth $639 billion, making Lehman's bankruptcy filing the largest in history.

Lehman Brothers' bankruptcy rocked the global economy. It was the fourth largest American investment bank at the time of its collapse, employing 25,000 people worldwide. The collapse of Lehman Brothers resulted in a credit freeze that brought the global financial system to the edge of complete collapse (*Investopedia2*, 2017).

One question most people never ask. Think about it. Money never disappears. When one person loses it, someone gains it. Who benefited from this huge financial meltdown in 2008? Did they see the collapse coming and prepared for it? Was it something similar to *The Big Short* movie? (ViralWhirl, 2016)

3.2 Alarming Factors for the Credit Card Bubble

Issuers have been pushing credit cards over the past few decades and they didn't slow down after the 2008 housing bubble burst. They have lowered their lending criteria, giving cards to subprime consumers in the same way that lenders issued mortgage loans to subprime borrowers. Let's take a look at the alarming factors for the credit card bubble in the U.S, U.K., Australia and China.

3.2.1 Factors for the Credit Card Bubble in the USA

The credit card debt situation in the USA has reached alarming proportions.

- The amount owed on credit cards hit the $1 trillion milestone in December 2016.

- By the end of October 2017 it was over $1.2 trillion (Golle, 2017). This is higher than the previous record of April 2008 when the United States had a collective $1.02 trillion in credit card debt (Lamagna, 2017).

- A recent credit card debt study by *Wallet Hub* confirms that Americans still owe more than a trillion dollars in credit card debt (Comoreanu, 2018).

- In March 2018 Americans' revolving debt, the bulk of which is credit card balances, hit $1.027 trillion (Herman, 2018).

- As previously stated in the Introduction, the total U.S. household credit card debt is currently approximately $1.03 (ValuePenguin, 2018).

After three quarter-point interest rate hikes by the Federal Reserve in 2017 and two more hikes thus far in 2018, consumers have to pay more interest charges than before. With underemployment and increases in food prices, medical care, and housing costs, it's not surprising that Americans are turning to their credit cards to meet their needs. While some consumers are forced by circumstances to rely on their credit cards, others simply lack discipline and use their cards to make unnecessary purchases.

While defaults are still below the 6.8% that happened during the last recession, one can expect consumers to default more as interest rates keep increasing. With over $20 trillion in national debt, the U.S. economy itself isn't looking too good and there are indicators that the USA might go into recession or, as some think, even a depression. The official unemployment rates look good but the true unemployment rate is much higher as stated earlier. This means that consumer earnings may not be sufficient for U.S. household needs. Hopefully, President Donald J. Trump can use his *art of the deal* and his recent tax cuts to rescue the U.S. economy and reduce its trillions in national debt (Trump & Schwartz, 2015).

3.2.2 Factors for the Credit Card Bubble in the UK, Australia and China

There is a danger that credit card bubbles may also burst in the U.K., Australia and perhaps even in China.

- As previously discussed in Chapter 2, the credit card situation is no better in the UK where some consumers are committing suicide because they cannot meet their credit card debt obligations. However, the Bank of England and financial regulatory agencies have taken an interest in the situation because they're worried about a possible recession and they're making an effort to curb the problem.

- In Australia, people are struggling to pay off their credit card debt and falling prey to unscrupulous lenders who simply exacerbate the problems. Luckily, the government is changing policy in order to protect consumers.

- In China, the problems have not yet become public, but people are already struggling with debt.

3.3 The Bursting Point

Credit cards debt isn't an isolated debt. Altogether, American consumers owe over $12.7 trillion in student loans, housing loans, car loans, credit cards, and other personal loans. With such a toxic mix of debt, it seems that our debt bubble could burst at any moment now.

3.3.1 American Debt As High Now As It Was At Height Of 2008 Credit Bubble

Americans now owe more money than they owed at the height of the credit bubble in 2008, just as the global financial system began to collapse (Corkery & Cowley, 2017). Therefore, compounding interest rates aren't limited to credit cards alone but to a wide range of loans, all of which have to be serviced and are increasingly becoming difficult to service.

A great possibility now exists that the ever-increasing interest rates on consumer loans can put many Americans back into a hole, prompting a new wave of defaults, much like the one that accompanied the mortgage meltdown a decade ago. Credit-card issuers have confirmed that write-offs rose drastically in 2017. At the end of the third quarter of 2017, CitiGroup, for example, reported that its credit card losses had risen by 36% to $611 million in the last year (Hardecopf, 2017).

The New York Federal Reserve has confirmed that percentage of credit card debt that was delinquent (over 90 days old) was 7.5% in November 2017 (Williams, 2017). By the end of January 2018 the percentage was down to 6% (Wolff-Mann, 2018) but the risk for lenders is still high, considering that 6% of $1 trillion amounts to $60 billion that might never be collected. That's a huge problem facing lenders! That is a huge problem facing the borrowers who might default. At the end of the second quarter of 2017, credit card delinquency rates for U.S. banks had risen to 2.47% from 2.20% a year earlier, according to New York Federal Reserve data (Subba & Lahiri, 2017).

3.3.2 Global Debt Time Bombs

The credit card business in the United States is in crisis, though most people aren't aware of this. But then, no one wanted to admit there was a mortgage bubble till it burst in 2008! Maybe it's too much to expect the authoritative economists to admit that the United States has a credit card debt time bomb. They probably prefer to act surprised when the bubble bursts.

In China, the credit card debt is becoming more serious, but the main problem is the national debt that might lead to an economic recession there. The recession will affect the consumers, who will then default on their personal debts, including the credit card debts, seriously affecting the lenders' stability. The recession will also affect nearly every country's economy, since China trades heavily with many countries.

By the looks of things, a global economic recession might begin in the U.S. with the bursting of the credit card bubble or in China with the collapse of the economy under a heavy sovereign debt.

Chapter 4:
Credit Card Debt Relief Solutions

Credit card debt is a huge risk for individual borrowers. The accumulating interest, late fees, and over-the-limit fees all add up on top of the principal, causing consumers to sink further into debt. It can be such a huge burden that people commit suicide because they don't see a way out of the debt crisis.

Consumers don't realize that cards are issued in order for lenders to make easy money by charging compound interest. While they work very hard for their money, consumers don't always understand the value of that money. Instead of safeguarding and investing their money, they may waste it by buying unnecessary goods. Instead of using money on hand, they prefer to spend money before they earn it. Then they pay interest on that loan. It only makes sense if there is a real emergency, but if credit cards are used for routine purchases, they're a waste of hard-earned money.

Consumers who owe a lot of money on credit cards are at risk of default. As previously discussed, the Federal Reserve Bank in the United States has increased interest rates several times in 2017, twice in 2018 and plans to keep increasing rates in the future. Soon, many credit card borrowers won't be able to meet their debt obligations and the credit card bubble will burst any time now. Higher interest rates will also affect mortgage loans, car loans, and student loans. Consumers will be stuck with a terrible credit history for a long time and won't be able to borrow at critical moments.

It's time for consumers to start getting out of credit card debt now!

4.1 Credit Card Delinquency

Credit cardholders have a contract to pay back the money that they borrow through the credit cards every month.

- When they miss a payment for a few days, they're delinquent.
- When they miss a month, they're 30 days delinquent.
- They're generally reported to credit bureaus after missing two consecutive payments, affecting their credit score.
- After missing four payments, the account can be turned over to debt collectors.
- After missing five payments, they can expect legal action, and use of the card may be suspended. (Papadimitriou, 2017)

To protect themselves, consumers are better off making the minimum payment on the card. For those who cannot manage any more, debt relief solutions are available.

4.2 Debt Consolidation

Debt consolidation is the grouping of all the various personal loans, such as credit card debt, student loans, and car loans, into one payment. The consumer ends up paying what he can afford every month without pressure from the various creditors. The consumer can arrange this with his bank or approach a not-for-profit organization for help. Debt consolidation restructures debts but doesn't eliminate any of them. Lower interest isn't guaranteed, and if a consumer gets lower interest, be aware that it can increase later. Also, lower monthly repayment means that a consumer will be paying the consolidated loan for a long time. There are several ways to do this, as discussed in the remainder of this chapter (Mecham, 2017).

4.2.1 Debt Consolidation Loan

The consumer takes out one lower-interest rate loan in order to pay off various debts, meaning that the consumer consolidates all the debts into one. The appeal of this loan lies in its lower monthly payment, which naturally extends the term of the loan. If the consumer keeps up the now affordable monthly payments, he will eventually get out of debt. All in all, the consumer pays much more than if he had stuck to repaying the old loans (*Debt.org1*).

4.2.2 Debt Management Plan

Debt management plans are run by non-profit organizations (NPO), which charge no (or low) fees and by for-profit organizations that charge high fees. They are regulated but how they are regulated differs from country to country. (Debt.org2)

- The plan starts with a credit counselling session to determine how much you can pay.

- The NPO negotiates with lenders for a lower interest rate and a waiver/reduction of late fees.

- Then you make one monthly payment to the NPO, which splits it among the creditors.

- In addition, you have to pay a monthly fee to the NPO for their services.

- After 3 to 5 years, you're free from debt and your credit score improves (*Debt.org1*).

The primary benefit of a debt management plan is that the late fees are reduced or waived. There's also the benefits of lower interest rates and not having to pay several different creditors. However, you still end up taking longer to pay off the loans and you could end up paying more.

4.2.3 Do it Yourself Consolidation

A cardholder who carries balances on multiple credit cards may consider a *Do It Yourself* consolidation plan by taking the following actions:

- Find a low-interest rate credit card and transfer all the balances owed on other cards. Just make sure that the transfer fee doesn't exceed the interest saved.

- Borrow from your pension fund (if one exists).

- Borrow equity from a refinanced housing loan (which happens to have a lower interest rate) to pay off the credit cards.

Please keep in mind that there may be a penalty and a tax charge when you borrow from your pension fund. Find out from your pension administrators how much is involved before borrowing (Mecham, 2017).

4.3 Debt Negotiation

Now let's look at "debt negotiation," also known as debt settlement, debt arbitration, or credit settlement. You and your creditor(s) agree on a reduced balance that will be regarded as payment in full. You're allowed to settle when you've

- Fallen behind in payment.
- Created a bad credit record.
- Genuinely don't earn enough to keep paying the full amount.

Let's consider the pros and cons of the debt negotiation process:

The Pros of Debt Negotiation: To begin the debt negotiation process, you approach a debt settlement company or a lawyer who advises you to stop paying your various creditors so that you look desperate (*YugeDebt,* 2017). The debt settlement company or lawyers deals directly with your creditor(s) – not you. More specifically, you start paying the debt settlement company until you have accumulated an amount large enough to negotiate with the creditor(s) so that they agree to settle. As a result, you pay far less than the original debt. Please note that the debt settlement company charges a fee for the service (O'Shea, 2017).

The Cons of Debt Negotiation: One problem is that debt negotiation may not always stop late fees, collection notices, or threats of being sued. Hence, this can be a painful process. Another problem is that when you stop paying, the creditor informs the credit bureau about your late payment and all the calls made to you. This damages your credit rating. When you finally settle, the credit bureau doesn't automatically erase your bad record, and you'll struggle to secure loans again. In fact, they may record the settlement as "Charged-Off Settled" or "Paid-Settled," which is very different from "Paid in Full." You'll have to painfully and slowly rebuild your credit score. The unforeseen problem is that you're expected to pay tax on the forgiven debt.

This method of debt relief has too many negative consequences. Be careful when you see ads from debt settlement companies promising you that you'll pay less.

4.4 Bankruptcy

If necessary, you have an option to file for bankruptcy! It is a legal route that consumers may take when they can no longer pay their debts. Bankruptcy reduces, restructures, or eliminates the debts.

In the United States, there are two types of bankruptcy: Chapter 7 and Chapter 13.

4.4.1 Chapter 7 (of the Bankruptcy Code)

Chapter 7 legally frees the debtor from the debt, and the creditors can no longer pursue the debts. The debtor is permitted to keep key assets that are considered "exempt property" and is instructed to sell "non-exempt property" to repay the debts. (Elias, 2017)

4.4.2 Chapter 13 (of the Bankruptcy Code)

Chapter 13 is for people who don't want to lose their property or don't qualify for Chapter 7 bankruptcy due to their high income. In this process, the debtor draws up a 3-5-year repayment plan for the creditors, and whatever cannot be paid within the given period is written off. (O'Neill, 2018)

4.4.3 Key Things to Know About the Bankruptcy Process

The consumer starts by petitioning the bankruptcy court to release them from liability for their debts. The judge and court trustee examine the assets and liabilities of the individual and decide whether to discharge those debts so they're no longer legally required to pay them. As agreed, the consumer liquidates his assets to pay the debts or creates a repayment plan. After being awarded bankruptcy, the consumer is free to make a fresh start (*Debt.org3*).

Bankruptcy can be denied by the courts.

- In 2016, 95.5% of the people who filed for Chapter 7 bankruptcy were freed from their debts, meaning that 4.5% were denied their petition.

- In the same year, just over 50% of Chapter 13 applicants had their debts discharged, and the other 50% were denied (*Debt.org3*).

Bankruptcy may prevent or delay foreclosure on a home or repossession of a car or wage garnishment and other legal actions that creditors use to collect debts. However, there is a price to pay because it definitely affects a consumer's credit rating and future ability to borrow.

Bankruptcy laws may vary from country to country. However, the effects are the same: a consumer gets a chance to start over.

4.5 Managing Your Credit Card Debt to Avoid Delinquency

If you're not yet delinquent, and you have a large balance, get rid of it as fast as you can. Life tends to change fast, and you may wake up one day and find that you cannot service that debt any more. The best you can do right now is to reduce that balance fast to avoid debt problems later and to reduce interest costs. If you're a family person, make sure your spouse knows that you have problems with your credit card(s) and, together, work to reduce the debt.

Here are some ways to manage your credit card debt to avoid delinquency and to hopefully live debt-free:

1. Create a budget.
2. Make a detailed list of your daily expenditures – down to the penny. One easy way to do this is, at the end of the day, record all of your expenses in an Excel spreadsheet, on Google Sheets, Quicken software, etc. (Harvey, 2015; Quicken, 2017).

3. Hold on to all sales receipts. They may come in handy for tax deductions, etc.

4. Prioritize your expenditures. Once you know where most of your money is going, you'll decide where to cut down.

5. If you can, get a 0% interest card and transfer your balance(s) to that card.

6. Alternatively, get a personal loan with a lower interest rate than your card(s) and use it to pay off the credit card debt. Then manage the personal loan while making sure that you don't use the cards again.

7. Negotiate with your card issuer for a lower interest rate.

8. Pay more than the minimum required but don't rush to buy more things. You'll find that if you pay more, you'll reduce your interest payment for the year.

9. Have a garage sale and get rid of things that are saleable that you're not using, such as electrical gadgets, electronic gadgets, books, paintings, and clothes, which will fetch you extra money that you can use to pay your credit card debt.

10. Ask for a raise if you feel that you genuinely deserve it. If you succeed in getting it, use the extra income to pay off your debt.

11. Take on a part-time job, work a few extra hours every week, and use all the money to pay off your balance. This may be something you love to do like tutoring kids on mathematics or pet sitting.

12. Cash in your credit card reward points. Use that cash to pay your credit card debt.

13. If you receive a tax refund, use it to pay your credit card debt.

14. Fix your credit score errors. Get a free copy of your credit report from www.annualcreditreport.com or www.freecreditreport.com/.

15. Be sure to report any errors found on your credit report. Correction of errors will improve your credit score and even earn you a reduced interest rate.

16. As you work systematically to reduce your debt, start with those cards that have the highest interest rates because, due to the miracle of compounding interest, these cards will accumulate debt at a faster rate.

17. You do not have to destroy your credit cards, nor do you need to close your account. Closing a credit card account can impact your credit score (McNay, 2018).

18. Instead, you can continue to use your credit cards for monthly purchases, making sure that you pay them off at the end of every month.

19. As long as you do not revolve your balance, your credit card can become your best friend and can help you rebuild your credit.

4.6 Outright Cancellation of 100% of Unsecured Debt?

There are times when a cardholder simply cannot pay a debt because of job loss, illness, or other life challenges. In that case, the card issuer can nullify the agreement and declare part or the whole amount to be forgiven. The cardholder is notified in the form of Form 1099-C, which effectively turns the amount owed from a loan to income.

Example: Say you owe $10,000 and you receive Form 1099-C cancelling the whole amount. Then you must report that $10,000 as income to the IRS and pay taxes on it. If the figure on the Form 1099-C is too high, then the issuer has probably added exorbitant amount of late fees and interest which far exceed the actual amount owed. If that happens then call the issuer and ask for a correct Form 1099-C (*CreditKarma*, 2018; Wright).

4.7 Stricter Credit Limits

You may want to give your children credit cards, but their expenditure can create huge problems for you. One way of controlling expenditure on credit cards is to make sure that all authorized users of your credit line have a limit. Few cards offer that option. American Express gives a credit card account holder of all its cards the power to set limits on authorized users. *Costco*

Anywhere Visa® Card by Citi also gives account holders that option. If you're a business, most business cards set spending limits for authorized users, which are usually employees (Karp, 2016).

Consider these few options if you want to empower your children while keeping their expenditure under control. That way, your kids at college can learn to manage their balance and live within the limits. If they hit their credit limit before the end of the month, they have to manage without the card or earn the extra money they need.

Right now, lenders aren't going to stop increasing your credit limits until the law stops them, so it's up to borrowers to be strict.

References

Amadeo, Kimberley, US Economy: Could the Great Depression Happen Again? The Balance, https://www.thebalance.com/could-the-great-depression-happen-again-3305685, 2017a.

Amadeo, Kimberley, US Economic Outlook: For 2017 and Beyond, The Balance, https://www.thebalance.com/us-economic-outlook-3305669, 2017b.

Amadeo, Kimberley, The Balance, What Caused the 2008 Global Financial Crisis? https://www.thebalance.com/what-caused-2008-global-financial-crisis-3306176, 2017c.

Amaro, Sylvia, CNBC, China's Debt Surpasses 300 Percent of GDP, IIF Says, Raising Doubts Over Yellen's Crisis Remarks, https://www.cnbc.com/2017/06/28/chinas-debt-surpasses-300-percent-of-gdp-iif-says-raising-doubts-over-yellens-crisis-remarks.html, 2017.

Andriotis A, America's Credit Card Tab Hits $1 Trillion, The Wall Street Journal, https://www.wsj.com/articles/the-nations-credit-card-tab-hits-1-trillion-1491593929?mod=e2fb, 2017

Barrow, Becky, Father Killed Himself Over Debt of £70,000 Run Up on 19 Credit Cards, The Telegraph, http://www.telegraph.co.uk/news/uknews/1456602/Father-killed-over-debt-of-70000-run-up-on-19-credit-cards.html, 2004.

Bartlett, Bruce, Who Saw the Housing Bubble Coming? Forbes, https://www.forbes.com/2008/12/31/housing-bubble-crash-oped-cx_bb_0102bartlett.html, 2009.

BBC, The Money Trap — How Banks Control the World Through Debt, YouTube, https://www.youtube.com/watch?v=Fg4VhALXgwE, 2012.

Bowsher, Ed, Credit Card Interest Rates Hit UK Consumers, Financial Times, https://www.ft.com/content/97493ef4-bf25-11e7-b8a3-38a6e068f464, 2017.

Britannica Encyclopedia, Credit Card, https://www.britannica.com/topic/credit-card

Chan, Szu Ping, Risky Lending Will Endanger Banks if Credit Bubble Bursts, Bank of England Warns, *The Telegraph*, http://www.telegraph.co.uk/business/2017/04/04/risky-lending-will-endanger-banks-credit-bubble-bursts-bank/, 2017.

Changzheng Hea, Bing Zhua, Mingzhu Zhanga, Xiaoli Heb, The Key Factors of Outstanding Credit Balances Among Revolvers: A Case Study of a Bank in China, http://ac.els-cdn.com/S1877050916312765/1-s2.0-S1877050916312765-main.pdf?_tid=9dbd7c64-7e89-11e7-be88-00000aacb35f&acdnat=1502451702_250f4dd4b3d2d9cac79b43a31a85475c, 2016.

Choudhry, Moorad and Suleman Baig, *The Mechanics of Securitization: A Practical Guide to Structuring and Closing Asset-Backed Security Transactions*, Wiley Finance, http://amzn.to/2BzkIiw, 2013.

Comoreanu, Alina, Credit Card Debt Study: Trends & Insights, *Wallet Hub*, https://wallethub.com/edu/credit-card-debt-study/24400/, 2018.

Corkery Michael and Stacy Cowley, Household Debt Makes a Comeback in the U.S., *The New York Times,* https://www.nytimes.com/2017/05/17/business/dealbook/household-debt-united-states.html, 2017.

CreditKarma, How to Cancel a Credit Card: The Do's and Don'ts Every Cardholder Should Know, https://www.creditkarma.com/credit-cards/i/how-to-cancel-credit-card/, March 2018.

Daily Mail Reporter, Suicide Over £100,000 Loan and Card Debt, *This Is Money* http://www.thisismoney.co.uk/money/cardsloans/article-1600371/Suicide-over-100000-loan-and-card-debt.html, 2006.

Debt Support Trust, Debt and Suicide, http://www.debtsupporttrust.org.uk/debt-advice/debt-and-suicide

Debt.org1, Debt Consolidation, https://www.debt.org/consolidation/

Debt.org2, Debt Management Plans, https://www.debt.org/management-plans/.

Debt.org3, What Happens When You File Bankruptcy? https://www.debt.org/bankruptcy/.

Desjardins, Jeff, INFOGRAPHIC: The 5,000-Year History of Consumer Credit, *Business Insider*, http://www.businessinsider.com/5000-year-history-of-consumer-credit-2017-8, August 30, 2017.

Dickler, Jessica, Credit Card Users Rack Up Over $1 Trillion in Debt, *CNBC,* https://www.cnbc.com/2017/02/17/credit-card-users-rack-up-over-1-trillion-in-debt.html, February 17, 2017.

Dickler, Jessica, Here's How the Fed Rate Hike Will Affect Your Finances, CNBC, https://www.cnbc.com/2018/06/13/heres-how-the-fed-rate-hike-will-affect-your-finances.html, 2018.

Dilworth, Kelly, Rate Survey: Average Card APR Surges to Record 16.06 Percent, http://www.creditcards.com/credit-card-news/interest-rate-report-7517-up-2121.php, 2017

Discover, How Does Credit Card Debt Affect the Economy? https://www.discover.com/credit-cards/resources/how-does-credit-card-debt-affect-the-economy, 2017.

Durden, Tyler, Record 95.9 Million Americans Are No Longer in the Labor Force, *ZeroHedge,* https://www.zerohedge.com/news/2018-06-01/record-959-million-americans-are-no-longer-labor-force, June 1, 2018.

Elias, Stephen, et. al., How to File for Chapter 7 Bankruptcy, Amazon Digital Services LLC, https://amzn.to/2JGjrgZ, 2017.

Elkins, Kathleen, Here's How Much the Average US Family Has in Credit Card Debt, *CNBC,* https://www.cnbc.com/2017/05/17/how-much-the-average-us-family-has-in-credit-card-debt.html, May 17, 2017.

Elliott, Larry, Bank of England Warns of Complacency Over Big Rise in Personal Debt, *The Guardian,* https://www.theguardian.com/business/2017/jul/24/bank-of-england-household-debt-bank-credit-card-car-loans, July 24, 2017.

Emmerton, K., Scott Morrison Tackles Australia's $52 Billion Credit Card Debt With Four New Reforms, *Mozo,* https://

mozo.com.au/credit-cards/articles/scott-morrison-tackles-australia-s-52-billion-credit-card-debt-with-four-new-reforms, June 2017.

Encyclopaedia Britannica, Credit Card, https://www.britannica.com/topic/credit-card

Federal Reserve, Prime Rate, https://www.fedsearch.org/board_public/search?text=prime+rate&Search=

Finder1, Australians' Household Debt Nears Highest Worldwide, https://www.finder.com.au/australias-personal-debt-reported-as-highest-in-the-world, 20 June 2017.

Finder2, Australian Credit Cards and Credit Card Statistics, https://www.finder.com.au/credit-cards/credit-card-statistics

Finder3, Australians' Household Debt Nears Highest Worldwide, https://www.finder.com.au/australias-personal-debt-reported-as-highest-in-the-world, December 17, 2017.

FRED, Delinquency Rates on Credit Card Loans, All Commercial Banks, Federal Reserve Economic Data, https://fred.stlouisfed.org/series/DRCCLACBS, 2018.

Frontline: Secret History of the Credit Card, http://amzn.to/2BhKsmA, 2004.

Giles, Chris, UK Credit Card Borrowing Grows at Fastest Pace in 11 Years, *Financial Times,* https://www.ft.com/content/972e11a0-45dc-11e7-8519-9f94ee97d996, 2017.

Global Blue, Chinese Millennials Embrace Credit-Card Debt, http://www.globalblue.com/corporate/market-insights/

business-insights/chinese-millennials-embrace-credit-card-debt/

Golle, V., Consumer Credit in U.S. Rises by Most Since November 2016, *Bloomberg*, https://www.bloomberg.com/news/articles/2017-11-07/consumer-credit-in-u-s-increases-by-most-since-november-2016, November, 2017.

Hardecopf, Bill, JPMorgan, Citigroup Expect More Credit Card Users to Default, *Forbes*, https://www.forbes.com/sites/billhardekopf/2017/10/13/this-week-in-credit-card-news-defaults-steadily-rising-google-teams-with-retailers-to-fight-amazon/#5b0e9fb147a3, October 2017.

Hart, William, Thomas Kidd, Lane Rettig, and Nicholas Walker, Consumer Credit in China, Wharton University of Pennsylvania, https://global.wharton.upenn.edu/consumer-credit-in-china/, January 2, 2014.

Hartmann, Thom, Derivatives Whiz Fired for Whistle Blowing About Frightening Trades, Thom Hartmann Talk Show, https://www.youtube.com/watch?v=ciiKONDAucc, 2009.

Harvey, Grey, *Excel 2016 All-in-One for Dummies*, http://amzn.to/2CSYXer, 2015.

Herman, Jeff, Credit Card Debt Statistics, CreditCards.com, https://www.creditcards.com/credit-card-news/credit-card-debt-statistics-1276.php, 2018.

Holt, Jeff, A Summary of the Primary Causes of the Housing Bubble and the Resulting Credit Crisis: A Non-Technical Paper, *Journal of Business Inquiry,* https://www.uvu.edu/woodbury/docs/summaryoftheprimarycauseofthehousingbubble.pdf, 2009.

Holy Bible, King James Version, Zondervan Publisher, http://amzn.to/2iXGd7c, 2010.

Influential Individuals, *Warren Buffett: The Life, Lessons & Rules for Success*, Amazon Digital Services LLC, http://amzn.to/2EZj9Mc, 2017.

Inman P., UK Credit Binge Approaching Levels Not Seen Since 2008 Crash, *The Guardian,* https://www.theguardian.com/business/2017/jan/04/uk-credit-cards-borrowing-debt-economic-crash-fears, 2017.

Investopedia1, When Did the Real Estate Bubble Burst? http://www.investopedia.com/ask/answers/100314/when-did-real-estate-bubble-burst.asp, 2016.

Investopedia2, Case Study: The Collapse of Lehman Brothers, http://www.investopedia.com/articles/economics/09/lehman-brothers-collapse.asp, 2017.

Janda, Michael, Credit Card Bankruptcies Could Be the Next Banking Scandal, *ABC News,* http://www.abc.net.au/news/2016-09-29/credit-cards-could-be-next-banking-scandal/7886276, 2016.

John, Alun, Chinese Banks Look to Credit Cards for Relief as Interest Income Under Pressure, *South China Morning Post,* http://www.scmp.com/business/banking-finance/article/2094566/chinese-banks-look-credit-cards-relief-interest-income, May 2017.

Karp, Gregory, Which Credit Cards Allow You to Set a Spending Limit for Authorized Users? *NerdWallet*, https://www.nerdwallet.com/blog/credit-cards/credit-card-spending-limit-for-authorized-users/, August 3, 2016.

Kilpatrick, Ryan, U.S. Credit Card Debt Tops $1 Trillion for the First Time Since the Recession, *Fortune,* http://www.pbs.org/wgbh/pages/frontline/shows/credit/more/rise.html, April 10, 2017.

Konsko, Lindsay, Do People in Other Countries Use Credit Cards as Much as Americans? *NerdWallet,* https://www.nerdwallet.com/blog/credit-cards/people-countries-credit-cards-americans/ 2014.

Lamagna, Maria, Americans Now Have the Highest Credit-Card Debt in U.S. History, *MarketWatch,* http://www.marketwatch.com/story/us-households-will-soon-have-as-much-debt-as-they-had-in-2008-2017-04-03, 2017.

Leuthold, Dave, 5 Ways Credit Card Debt Affects the US Economy, *Debt Management Advice.,* http://www.centuryni.com/blog/5-ways-credit-card-debt-affects-us-economy/, 2017.

Li, C., China's Recent Efforts to Deal With Stressed Loans, *Pacific Exchange Blog,* https://www.frbsf.org/banking/asia-program/pacific-exchange-blog/china-recent-efforts-stressed-loans/, June, 2017.

Luthi, Ben, 5 Personal Loans with Incredibly Low Interest Rates, *Student Loan Hero,* https://studentloanhero.com/featured/low-interest-personal-loans-best/, 2017.

Macfarlane, Alec, China Has a Huge Debt Problem: How Bad Is It? *CNN Money,* http://money.cnn.com/2017/05/25/news/economy/china-debt-economy/index.html, 2017a.

Macfarlane, Alec, Moody's Cuts China Debt Rating for First Time Since 1989, *CNN Money,* http://money.cnn.

com/2017/05/23/investing/china-debt-downgrade/index. html?iid=EL, 2017b.

Mack, Iris, *U. S. Debt: $800,000+ per Family? Trillions? Quadrillions?*, Amazon Createspace, http://amzn. to/2B0WFbt, 2017a.

Mack, Iris, *Wall Street Options Strategy: Everyone Can Learn Covered Calls* (Chinese Edition), Amazon Createspace, https://amzn.to/2LIKm8y 2017b.

Mack, Iris, *Rescate de Wall Street Para Main Street: La Estrategia Blindala Que Sera' Bien Pagada* (Spanish Edition), Amazon Createspace, https://amzn.to/2sTep6i 2017c.

Mack, Iris, *A Wall Street Bailout for Main Street,* Amazon Createspace, http://amzn.to/2CHcG6F, 2016.

Mack, Iris, *Energy Trading and Risk Management: A Practical Approach to Hedging, Trading and Portfolio Diversification,* Wiley Finance Publishers, https://amzn.to/2HKfKRs, 2014.

Mack, Iris, *Mama Says, "Money Doesn't Grow on Trees!",* Amazon Createspace, https://amzn.to/2y7Exj8, 2011.

Mack, Iris, *Mama Says, "Money Doesn't Grow on Trees!",* Amazon Createspace, https://amzn.to/2touGWs, 2004.

McAleenan, Tim, Andrew Kahr: The Man Responsible for High Credit Card Fees, Interest Rates, and Corrupt Business Practices, *The Conservative Income Investor*, http:// theconservativeincomeinvestor.com/2014/02/16/andrew-kahr-the-man-responsible-for-high-credit-card-fees-interest-rates-and-corrupt-business-practices/, 2014.

McCulloch, Michael, Personal Debt in Australia 4th Highest in the World, *Debt Collection News*, http://www.lcollect.com.au/news-blog/personal-debt-in-australia-4th-highest-in-the-world, June 29, 2017.

McNay, Shannon, Does Closing a Credit Card Hurt Your Credit Score and Should You Do It?, *My Bank Tracker*, https://www.mybanktracker.com/credit-cards/faq/pros-cons-canceling-vs-cutting-credit-cards-134746, 2018.

Mecham, Jesse, *The Debt Consolidation Myth: A Proven Method to Help You Get Out of Debt While Still Living Your Life*, Amazon Digital Services LLC, http://amzn.to/2CF0S8t, 2017.

Milligan, Brian, BBC News, Consumers warned as credit card rates hit 10-year high, https://www.bbc.com/news/business-41733925, November 24, 2017.

MoneySmart, Credit Card Debt Clock, *ASIC's MoneySmart*, https://www.moneysmart.gov.au/borrowing-and-credit/credit-cards/credit-card-debt-clock, July 30, 2017.

Morrell, Alex, Americans Are Suddenly Defaulting on Their Credit Cards, *Business Insider UK*, http://uk.businessinsider.com/credit-card-defaults-have-spiked-as-lending-standards-fall-2017-6, June 9, 2017.

O'Neill, Cara, Chapter 13 Bankruptcy: Keep Your Property & Repay Debts Over Time, NOLO, https://amzn.to/2t1SHxe, 2018.

O'Shea, Bev, How Does Debt Settlement Work? *NerdWallet*, https://www.nerdwallet.com/blog/finance/how-does-debt-settlement-work/, 2017.

Oyedele, Akin, More Americans are Struggling to Pay Their Credit Cards, and What's Holding Them Back is Only Getting Worse, Business Insider, http://www.businessinsider.com/credit-card-late-payments-and-interest-rates-rise-2018-5, 2018.

Pak, Nataly, Credit Card Debt Surpasses $1 Trillion in the U.S. for First Time, *ABC News,* https://abcnews.go.com/Business/credit-card-debt-surpasses-trillion-us-time/story?id=53608548, 2018.

Papadimitriou, Odysseas, Investopedia, How Credit Card Delinquency Works, https://www.investopedia.com/articles/pf/11/intro-to-credit-card-delinquency.asp, October 21, 2017.

PositiveMoney, Financial Crises and Recessions, http://positivemoney.org/issues/recessions-crisis/

PYMNTS, Overdue Credit Card Payments in China on the Rise, *PYMNTS News,* http://www.pymnts.com/news/international/2016/overdue-credit-card-payments-china/, September 9, 2016.

Quicken Deluxe 2018 Release – 27-Month Personal Finance & Budgeting Membership, http://amzn.to/2CVeWsm, 2017.

Quinn, Michael, Money Expert, UK Personal Debt Levels Continue to Rise, https://www.moneyexpert.com/debt/uk-personal-debt-levels-continue-rise/. March 23, 2018.

Randall, David, How Credit Cards Hurt the Economy, *Forbes,* https://www.forbes.com/sites/moneybuilder/2010/04/27/how-credit-cards-hurt-the-economy/#ad65a59446e2, April 27, 2010.

Ross, Sean, When Did People First Start Using Collateral to Secure Loans? *Investopedia,* http://www.investopedia.com/ask/answers/032715/when-did-people-first-start-using-collateral-secure-loans.asp, 2015.

Rounds, Hannah, Average Household Credit Card Debt in the U.S. in 2018, Magnify Money, https://www.magnifymoney.com/blog/news/u-s-credit-card-debt-by-the-numbers628618371/, 2018.

Sandberg, Erica, 7 Things You Must Know About Credit Cards, *CreditCard.com,* http://www.creditcards.com/credit-card-news/help/7-things-to-know-about-credit-cards-6000.php, 2017.

Schoen, John, The May Jobs Report Is Great News for Everyone – Except Democrats Running for Office, *CNBC,* https://www.cnbc.com/2018/06/01/may-jobs-numbers-are-bad-news-for-democrats.html, 2018.

Shakespeare, William, *The Merchant of Venice*, Palala Press, http://amzn.to/2wBfXm1, 2015.

Shen, Lucinda, Warren Buffett Just Unloaded $195 Million Worth of These "Weapons of Mass Destruction, *Fortune,* http://fortune.com/2016/08/08/mass-destruction-buffett-derivatives/, 2016.

Sherman, Matthew, A Short History of Financial Deregulation in the United States, Center for Economic and Policy Research, http://cepr.net/documents/publications/dereg-timeline-2009-07.pdf, 2009.

Smith, William, Smith's Bible Dictionary: More than 6,000 Detailed Definitions, Articles, and Illustrations, Thomas Nelson Publisher, http://amzn.to/2w0tK3L, 2004.

Smith, Yves, The Chinese Debt Time Bomb, *Naked Capitalism,* https://www.nakedcapitalism.com/2017/07/chinese-debt-time-bomb.html, 2017.

Stein, Robin, The Ascendancy of the Credit Card Industry, *Frontline,* http://www.pbs.org/wgbh/pages/frontline/shows/credit/more/rise.html, 2004.

Steiner, Sheyna, The Evolution of Credit Cards, *Bankrate,* https://www.bankrate.com/finance/financial-literacy/the-evolution-of-credit-cards-1.aspx, 2008.

Subba, Nikhil and Diptendu Lahiri, Rising Credit Card Delinquencies to Add to U.S. Banks' Worries, https://www.reuters.com/article/us-usa-creditcards-delinquencies/rising-credit-card-delinquencies-to-add-to-u-s-banks-worries-idUSKCN1BQ2E0, September, 2017.

Taylor, David, Australia's Household Debt Crisis Is Worse Than Ever as Bills Pile Up and Wages Flatline, *ABC,* http://www.abc.net.au/news/2017-04-05/australias-household-debt-crisis-is-worse-than-ever/8413612, April 4, 2017.

The Economist, Just Spend, https://www.economist.com/news/finance-and-economics/21710292-chinas-consumer-credit-rating-culture-evolving-fastand-unconventionally-just, 2016.

Trump, Donald J. and Tony Schwartz, *Trump: The Art of the Deal,* Ballantine Books, http://amzn.to/2EYApB9, 2015.

ValuePenguin, https://www.valuepenguin.com/average-credit-card-debt, 2018.

ViralWhirl, *The Big Short* Movie Explained, https://www.youtube.com/watch?v=UFlHwkiAmyU, 2016.

Wallace, Tim, Is UK Heading Towards Another Credit Crisis? Bank Warning Over Boom in Car Loans and Card Debt, *The Telegraph,* http://www.telegraph.co.uk/business/2017/06/27/bank-england-orders-banks-hold-extra-114bn-emergencies/, June 28, 2017a.

Wallace, Tim, Household Debt to Hit Record High as Credit Card Splurge Adds Up, *The Telegraph,* http://www.telegraph.co.uk/business/2017/05/24/household-debt-hit-record-high-credit-card-spluge-adds/, 2017b.

Warwick-Ching, Lucy, Why Is Consumer Debt Hitting Headlines? *Financial Times,* https://www.ft.com/content/f6992568-4149-11e7-9d56-25f963e998b2, May 31, 2017.

Watson, Leon, Chinese Family of Three Commit Suicide After Racking Up £900 Credit Card Debt With No Means of Paying It Back, *Mailonline,* http://www.dailymail.co.uk/news/article-2649680/Chinese-family-three-commit-suicide-racking-900-credit-card-debt-no-means-paying-back.html, 2014.

Wikipedia1, History of Banking, https://en.wikipedia.org/wiki/History_of_banking

Wikipedia2, Andrew Kahr, https://en.wikipedia.org/wiki/Andrew_Kahr

Williams, Fred, Creditcards.com, NY Fed: Credit card delinquencies continue to rise, https://www.creditcards.com/credit-card-news/credit-card-delinquencies-rising-federal-reserve-household-debt-report.php, November 14, 2017.

Wolff-Mann, Ethan, Yahoo Finance, American credit card delinquencies are up, https://finance.yahoo.com/

news/american-credit-card-delinquencies-203127373. html?guccounter=1, May, 2018.

Wood, Callum, Australia's Household Debt Crisis, *The Trumpet*, https://www.thetrumpet.com/15939-australias-household-debt-crisis, June 2016.

Wright, Tiffany, What Is Credit Card Cancellation? https://budgeting.thenest.com/credit-card-debt-cancellation-27877.html

YugeDebt, Stock Market Secrets That Wall Street Doesn't Want You to Know: Debt Relief, https://www.yugedebt.com/ stock-market-secrets-wall-street-doesnt-want-know-debt-relief/, September 2017.

Index

www.ingramcontent.com/pod-product-compliance
Lightning Source LLC
Chambersburg PA
CBHW071225220526
45468CB00002B/740